READING POWER

Writing in the Ancient World

MAYAN WRITING IN MESOAMERICA

JIL FINE

The Rosen Publishing Group's
PowerKids Press™
New York

Published in 2003 by The Rosen Publishing Group, Inc.
29 East 21st Street, New York, NY 10010

First Edition

Book Design: Michael DeLisio

Photo Credits: Cover © Newberry Library, Chicago/SuperStock, Inc., pp. 4, 10 Werner Forman/Art Resource, NY; pp. 5 (top), 11 © SEF/Art Resource, NY; p. 5 (bottom) Michael DeLisio; p. 6 © A.K.G., Berlin, SuperStock, Inc.; pp. 6–7 © Charles & Josette Lenars/Corbis; p. 8 © SuperStock, Inc.; pp. 9, 15 © The Lowe Art Museum, The University of Miami/SuperStock, Inc.; p. 12 © North Wind Pictures Archive; pp. 13, 17 ©Art Resource, NY; pp. 16, 18, 19 © Scala/Art Resource, NY; pp. 20–21 © Ken Welsh/The Bridgeman Art Library, NY.

Library of Congress Cataloging-in-Publication Data

Fine, Jil.
Mayan writing in Mesoamerica / Jil Fine.
 p. cm. — (Writing in the ancient world)
Summary: Explores the development and use of written languages among the ancient Mayan people, who lived in an area comprised of Mexico, Central America, and part of South America known as Mesoamerica.
Includes bibliographical references and index.
ISBN 0-8239-6511-2 (lib. bdg.)
1. Mayan languages—Writing—Juvenile literature. [1. Mayan languages—Writing. 2. Hieroglyphics. 3. Writing—History. 4. Mayas.]
I. Title. II. Series.
F1435.3.W75 F55 2003
497'.415—dc21

                              2002002941

Contents

MESOAMERICA

Mesoamerica *(meh-zoh-uh-MAIR-ih-kuh)* was the land of southern Mexico and northern Central America. People have lived in Mesoamerica since about 21,000 B.C. Several civilizations began in ancient Mesoamerica between 1500 B.C. and 900 B.C. These civilizations had temples, art, and their own way of writing.

The Olmecs had the first civilization in Mesoamerica. This large stone monument is believed to be a likeness of one of their rulers.

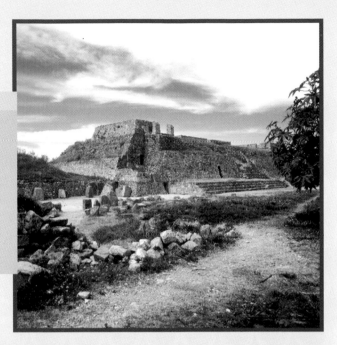

These are the remains of a Zapotec palace in the City of the Temples in southeastern Mexico.

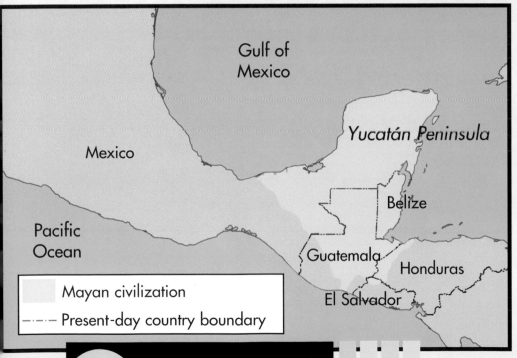

Gulf of Mexico

Yucatán Peninsula

Mexico

Belize

Pacific Ocean

Guatemala

Honduras

El Salvador

Mayan civilization

---·--- Present-day country boundary

The ancient Maya lived in Mesoamerica.

The Maya had one of the most advanced civilizations in Mesoamerica. They were farmers and had villages as early as 1500 B.C. Maize, or corn, was a very important crop. They also grew peppers, beans, cotton, and squash. The Maya had large cities with temples, palaces, and courts for playing ball.

Mayan temple in Mexico

The Mayan civilization had about 40 cities. These temples built by the ancient Maya are in present-day Guatemala.

The Maya had a calendar with 365 days. There were 18 months of 20 days each. Five days were added at the end of the calendar year.

MAYAN WRITING

The Maya had their own system of writing. Their writing system used more than 800 different hieroglyphs. Hieroglyphs were pictures that stood for objects, sounds, or ideas. Many hieroglyphs had more than one meaning. For example, a hieroglyph that looked like the sun could mean "sun." But it could also be used to mean "warmth."

Some Mayan hieroglyphs were carved in stone.

Some hieroglyphs stood for the sounds of words. The Maya sometimes used several hieroglyphs to spell out a word by its sounds.

Today, we still cannot read some of the ancient Mayan writings because each hieroglyph can have many different meanings.

The ancient Maya wrote about many things. They wrote stories about their wars and other important events, such as marriages and births. The Maya also wrote about the planets and stars that they studied. They often wrote about their religion, too.

This scene shows a Mayan soldier getting the things he needs for battle from his wife. The writing at the top says that it happened in A.D. February 12, 724.

This Mayan painting shows a war. The Maya sometimes painted pictures of the things they wrote about.

11

The Maya thought that writing was a gift from their gods. Only highly trained scribes wrote and read the Mayan hieroglyphs. The Maya believed that people who could write had a special power that let them talk to the Mayan gods. The Maya often carved their writings into stone or wood monuments and buildings.

The Maya carved hieroglyphs into tall, stone columns.

The Maya used hammers and sharp tools to carve their writings into stone walls.

13

The Maya also painted their writing on walls, pottery, and paper. They made paper out of fig tree bark or deer's skin. The Maya used porcupine quill brushes to write on the paper. The paper was folded to make a book, called a codex.

Hieroglyphs in Mayan codices were painted in colored ink. Book covers were made of jaguar skin.

The Maya painted their writing on the outside of pottery, such as this bowl.

THE FOUR CODICES

The Mayan civilization continued in Mesoamerica for hundreds of years. However, Spain took over the lands where the Maya lived around A.D. 1540. The Spanish destroyed most of the Mayan codices. Only four codices are known to exist today.

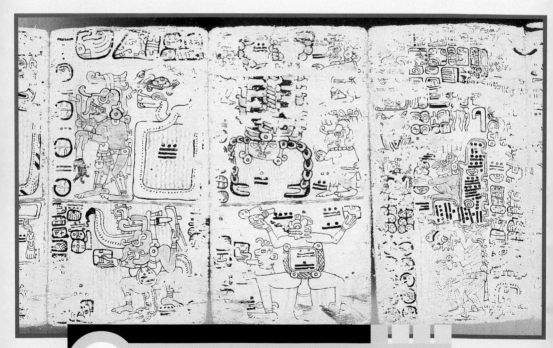

These are pages from the Madrid Codex, which contains religious writings.

On this section of the Dresden Codex, the Maya wrote about a moon goddess.

The four Mayan codices that remain have writings about religion, the stars and planets, and the Mayan calendar. They are between 20 and 112 pages long. The last codex was found in 1971 in a cave in Chiapas, Mexico.

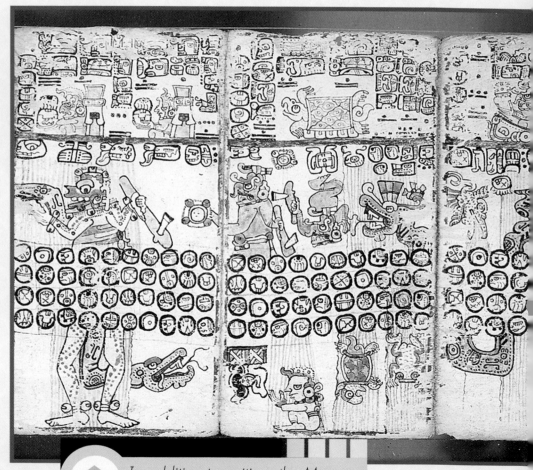

In addition to writing, the Maya often drew pictures in the codices.

CHECK IT OUT

▶ The codices are written in Yucatec. Yucatec is one of 31 Mayan languages.

Mayan hieroglyphs often looked like human faces and animals.

LEARNING FROM MAYAN WRITING

Scientists have learned much about the Maya from studying their writing. They have learned about Mayan wars, leaders, and religion. Scientists continue to study ancient Mayan writing. They hope to learn more about the Mayan civilization of Mesoamerica.

Many ancient Mayan buildings are still standing.

Glossary

carve (**kahrv**) to cut into something with great care

civilization (sihv-uh-luh-**zay**-shuhn) a way of life that includes cities, written forms of language, and special kinds of work for people

codex (**koh**-dehks) an ancient Mayan book

codices (**koh**-duh-seez) more than one codex

columns (**kahl**-uhmz) tall, narrow posts

hieroglyph (**hy**-ruh-glihf) a picture that stands for a word, idea, or sound

jaguar (**jag**-wahr) a large cat from Central and South America

porcupine (**por**-kyuh-pyn) an animal with quills

quill (**kwihl**) one of the long, sharp, hollow, needle-like hairs on a porcupine

religion (rih-**lihj**-uhn) the belief in a god and the practice of praying to that god

religious (rih-**lihj**-uhs) having to do with a system of faith or belief

scribes (**skrybz**) people who knew how to read and write in Mesoamerica

Resources

Books

Find Out About the Aztecs & Maya
by Fiona Macdonald
Southwater Publishing (2001)

The Mystery of the Maya:
Uncovering the Lost City of Palenque
by Peter Lourie
Boyds Mills Press (2001)

Web Sites

Due to the changing nature of Internet links, PowerKids
Press has developed an online list of Web sites related
to the subjects of this book. This site is updated regularly.
Please use this link to access the list:

http://www.powerkidslinks.com/waw/meso/

Index

Word Count: 483

Note to Librarians, Teachers, and Parents

If reading is a challenge, Reading Power is a solution! Reading Power is perfect for readers who want high-interest subject matter at an accessible reading level. These fact-filled, photo-illustrated books are designed for readers who want straightforward vocabulary, engaging topics, and a manageable reading experience. With clear picture/text correspondence, leveled Reading Power books put the reader in charge. Now readers have the power to get the information they want and the skills they need in a user-friendly format.